How to Draw
Insects

Barbara Soloff Levy

Dover Publications, Inc.
Mineola, New York

Bibliographical Note

How to Draw Insects is a new work, first published by Dover Publications, Inc., in 1999.

International Standard Book Number

ISBN-13: 978-0-486-47830-2
ISBN-10: 0-486-47830-0

Manufactured in the United States by Courier Corporation
47830002   2013
www.doverpublications.com

Note

Insects are fascinating creatures. Many are strange looking and fun to draw. They live everywhere in the world—from tangled rain forests to open grasslands, from deserts to swamps. The oldest insect group is the cockroach: it dates back 350 million years.

Some insects are harmful and can damage our crops and plants, the wood in our homes, and even our clothes, by eating them. Others are beneficial. They help us by eating the harmful ones, by pollinating our plants, and by being a source of food for many small animals.

Spiders, scorpions, and ticks are not insects. They belong to a group called arachnids. They have four pairs of legs; insects have six pairs. Also, insects have antennae and arachnids do not.

In this How to Draw book are just a few of the many kinds of insects and arachnids. Have fun making up your own creepy-crawly creatures by mixing up the different heads, bodies, and legs. Make them scary. Enjoy yourself!

There are three, four, or five drawings on each page. You start with simple shapes and then add to them. *(The dotted lines mean that you should erase that line.)* The last step shows you the final drawing in detail.

Start your drawing in pencil, because it is easy to erase. Then go over it with a felt-tip pen and color it. If you're not pleased with your drawing at first, keep trying. Artists redo their drawings many times before they complete the final one. You can trace each step first, to get the feel of how to draw the creature. Then try it on your own.

Drawing is fun. Be creative and remember to use your imagination.

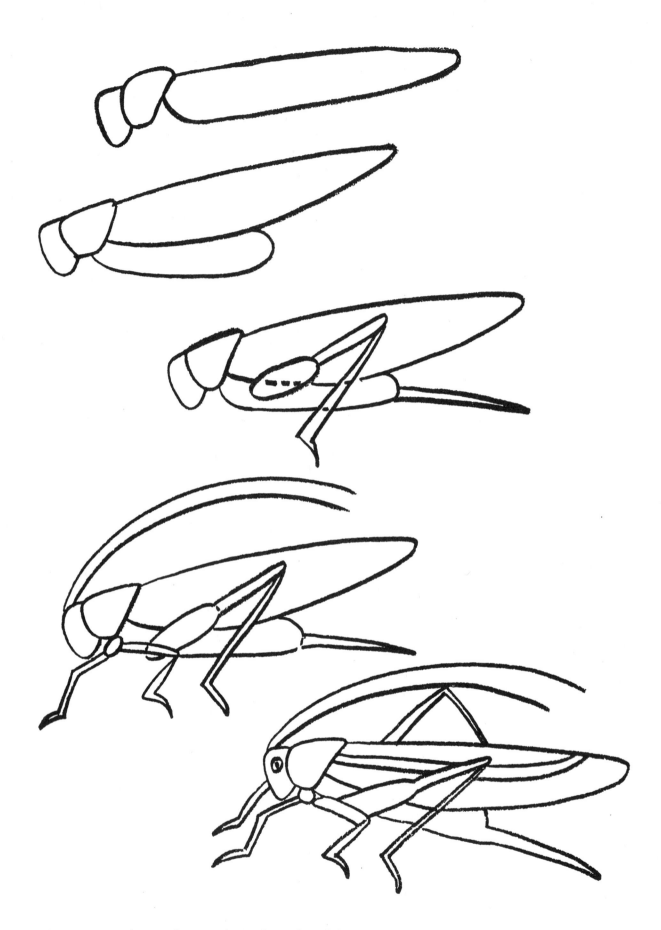

A **grasshopper** has a large head, big eyes, and long antennae.
Color it green or light brown.

Practice Page

Practice Page

Monarch butterflies are orange, black, and white.
They migrate south in the autumn.

Practice Page

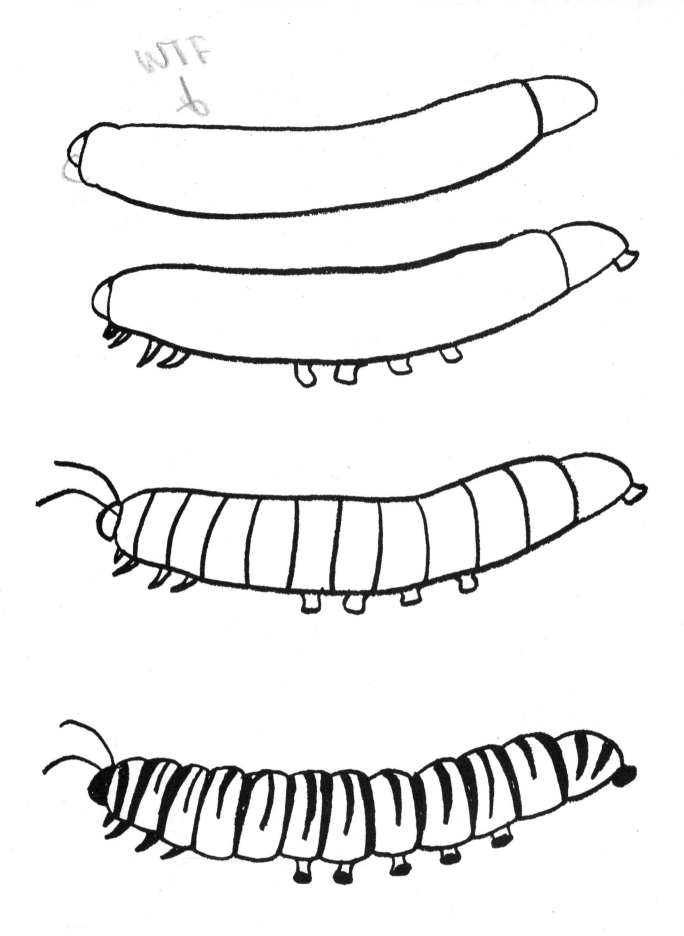

This **caterpillar** will emerge from its cocoon as a monarch butterfly.

Swallowtail butterflies, named for their distinctive tail,
usually are black and yellow.

8

Practice Page

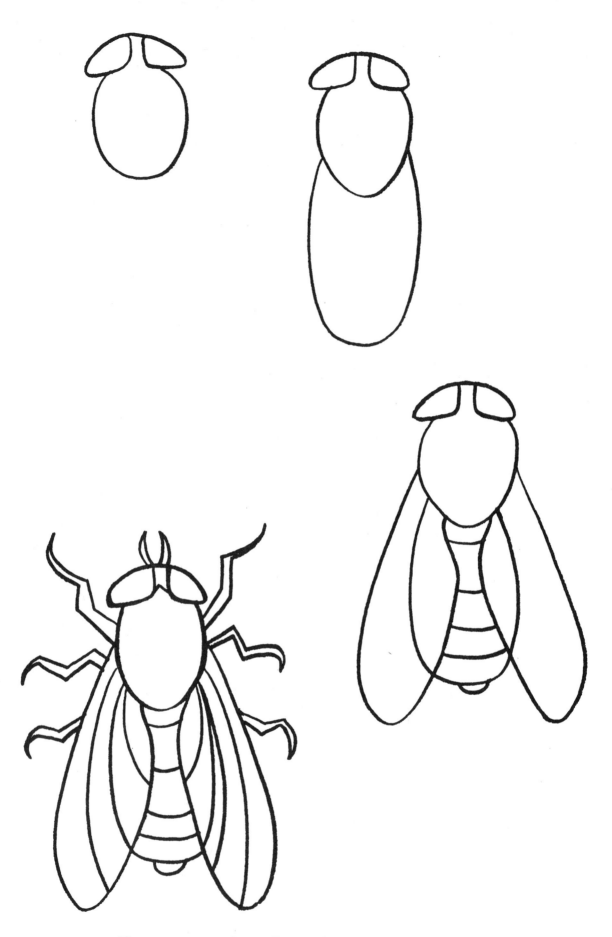

The ever-present **housefly** eats fruit and decaying matter
and can cause health problems by spreading diseases.
It is gray and partly yellowish, with black stripes and marks.

10

Practice Page

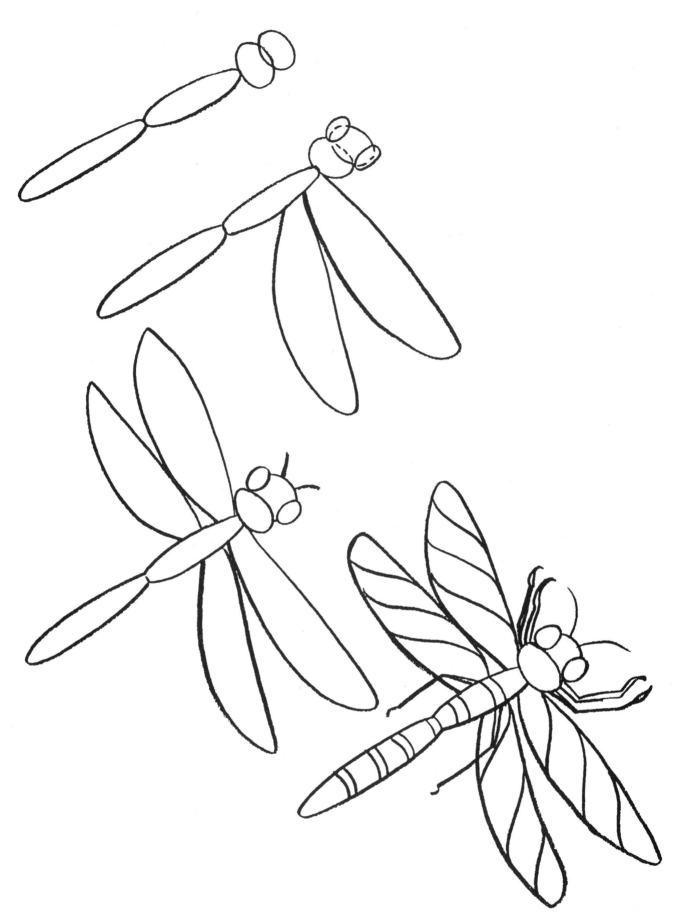

Dragonflies live near ponds and in moist meadows.
They are green. The largest, fastest-flying dragonflies
are called darners or darning needles.

12

Practice Page

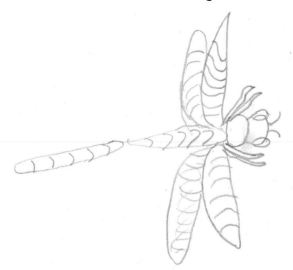

Tarantulas are poisonous spiders. They are brown or black.
Some have a leg span of almost 6 inches.

14

Practice Page

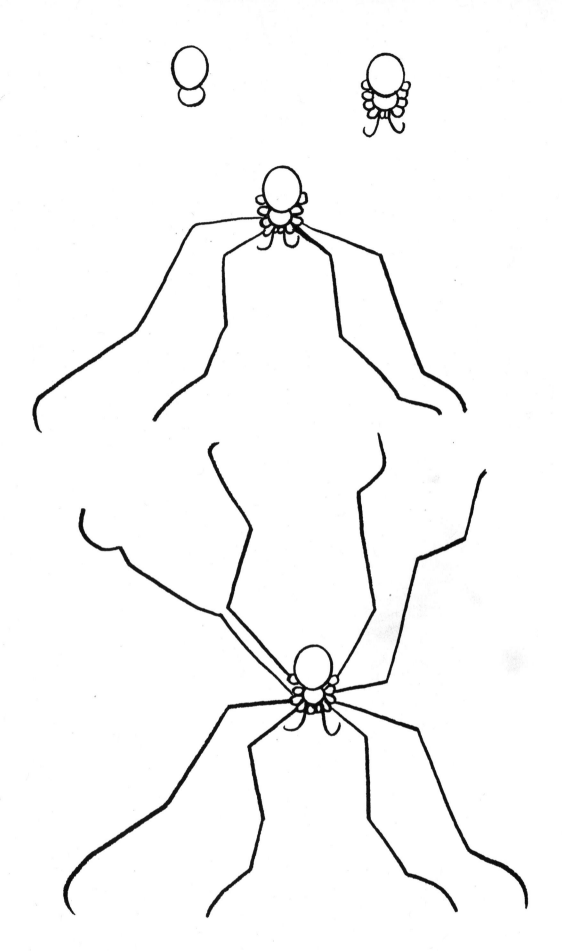

Daddy-long-legs spiders, also known as harvestmen, are light brown.
They hunt insects and worms, often at night.

Practice Page

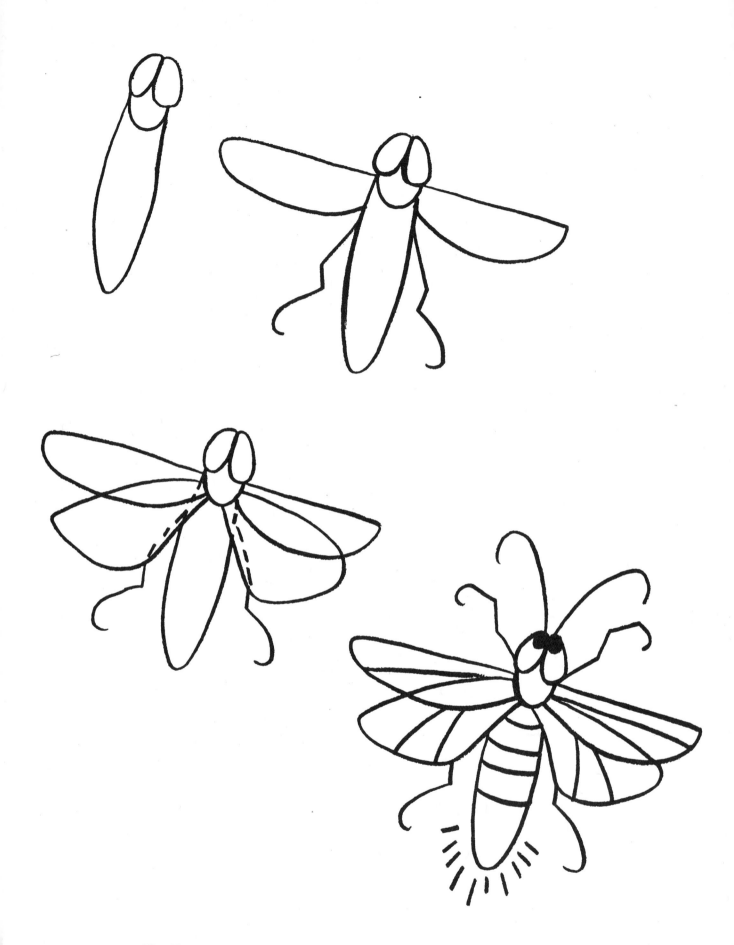

Fireflies actually are beetles—orange, black, and yellow in color. Their glow is emitted by light-producing tissue at the end of their abdomen.

Practice Page

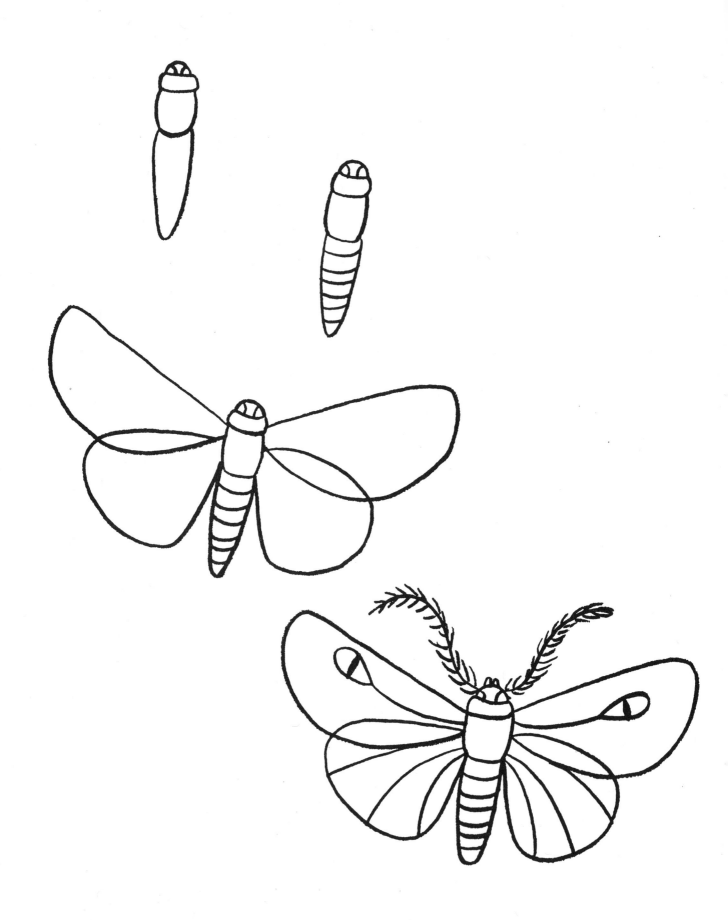

Many **moths** have feathery antennae. They differ from butterflies
in that they hold their wings horizontal when resting.
Color this one with bright oranges and yellows.

Practice Page

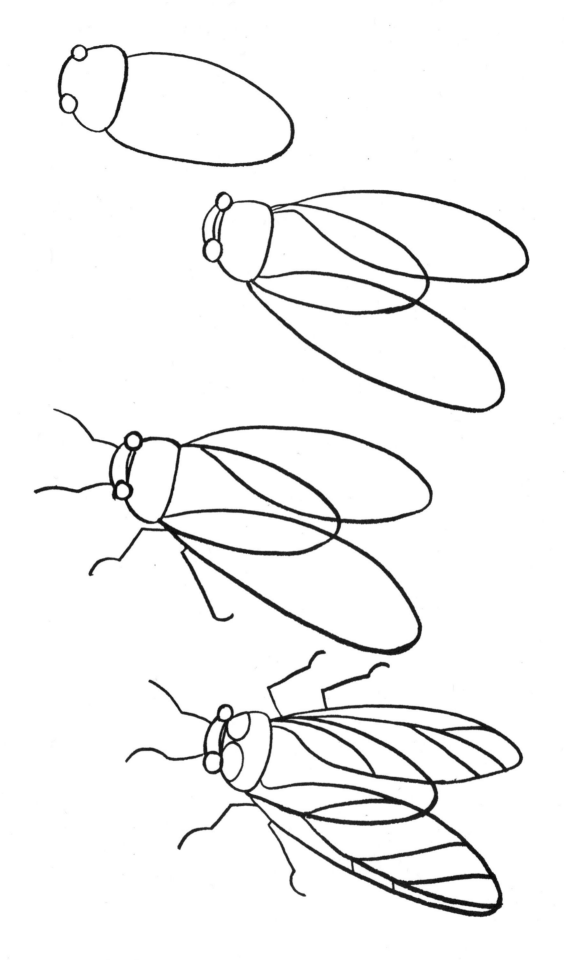

Green-and-brown **cicadas** hum in the grass during summer.

Practice Page

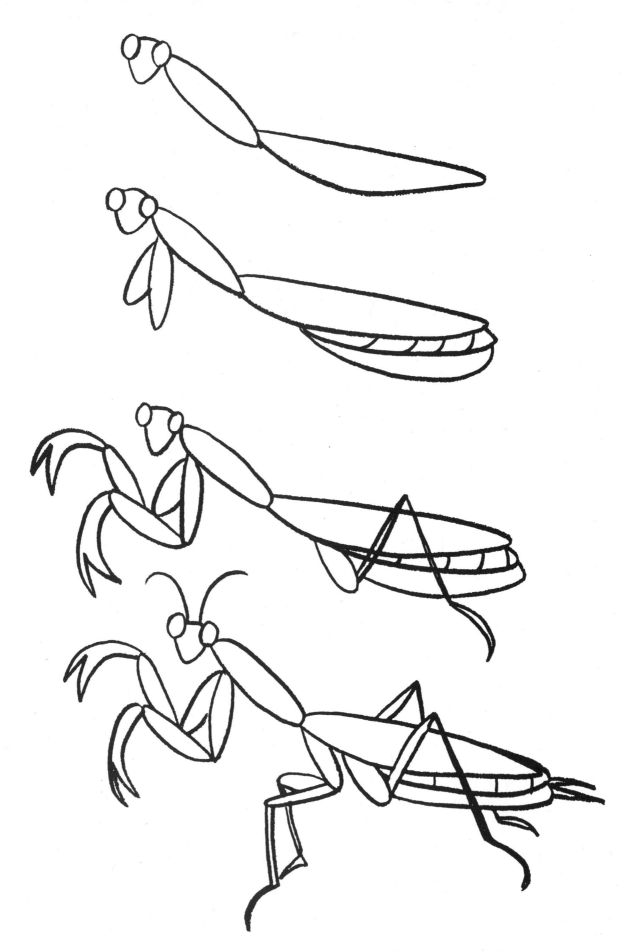

The **praying mantis** eats many insect pests that damage gardens.
It is green and uses its large front legs to capture its food.

24

Practice Page

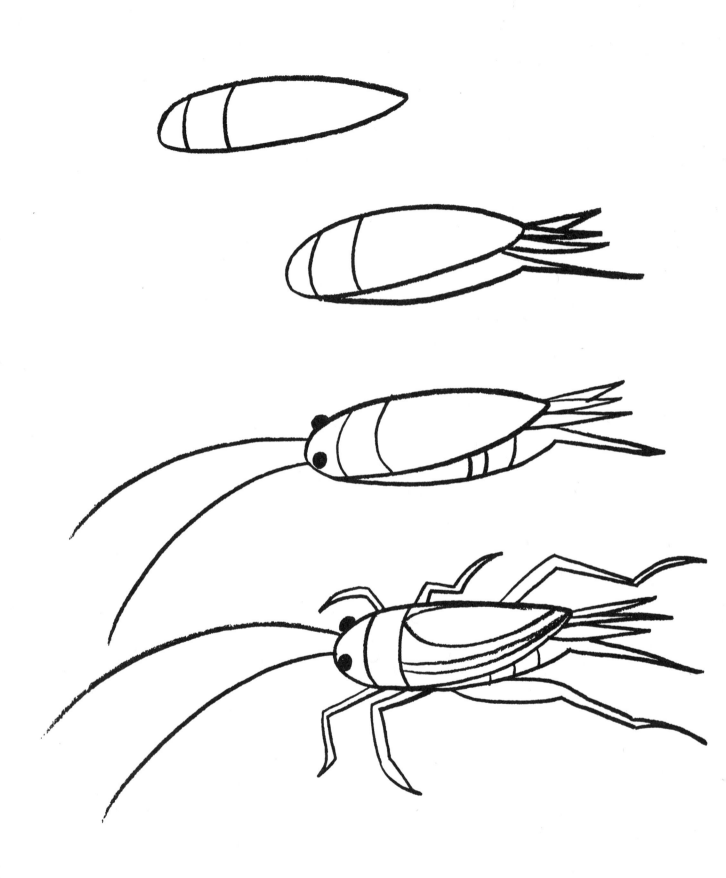

Crickets may be green, brown, or black.
They can be heard chirping loudly on summer nights.

Practice Page

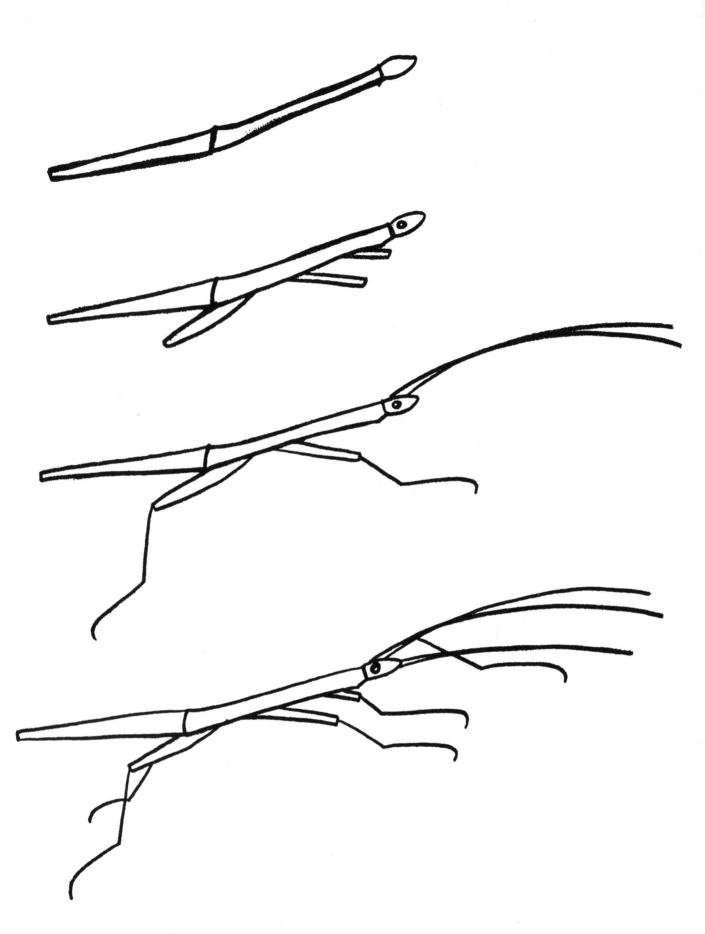

The **walkingstick,** a brown insect, takes advantage of camouflage to survive. When it is on a tree, it looks like a twig without leaves.

Practice Page

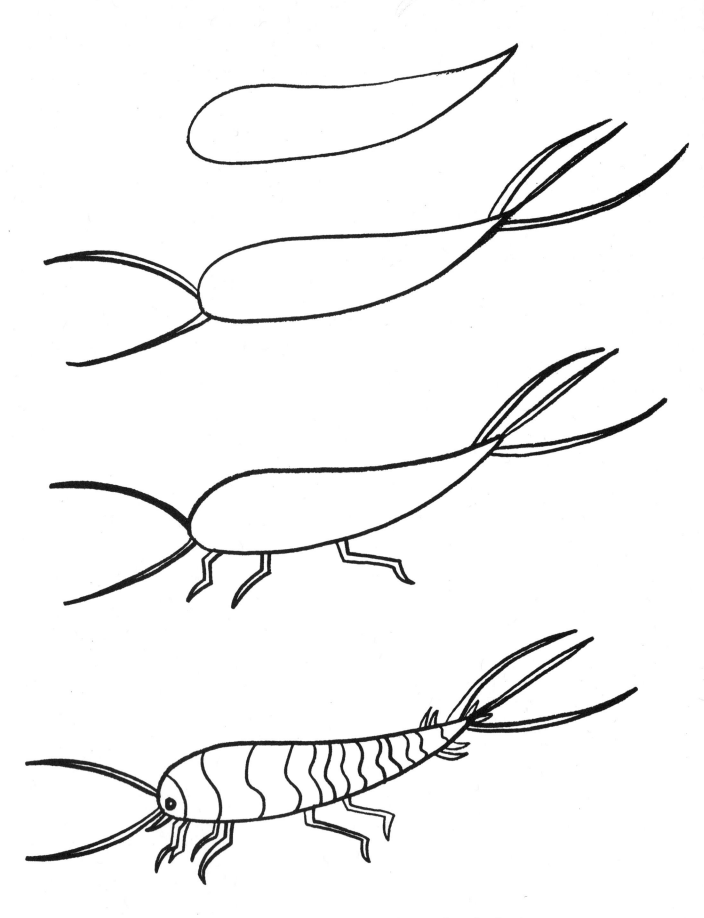

Silverfish have tiny, silvery scales on their bodies.
They live indoors in dark, warm places and move about quickly.
Sometimes they are seen in bathtubs.

30

Practice Page

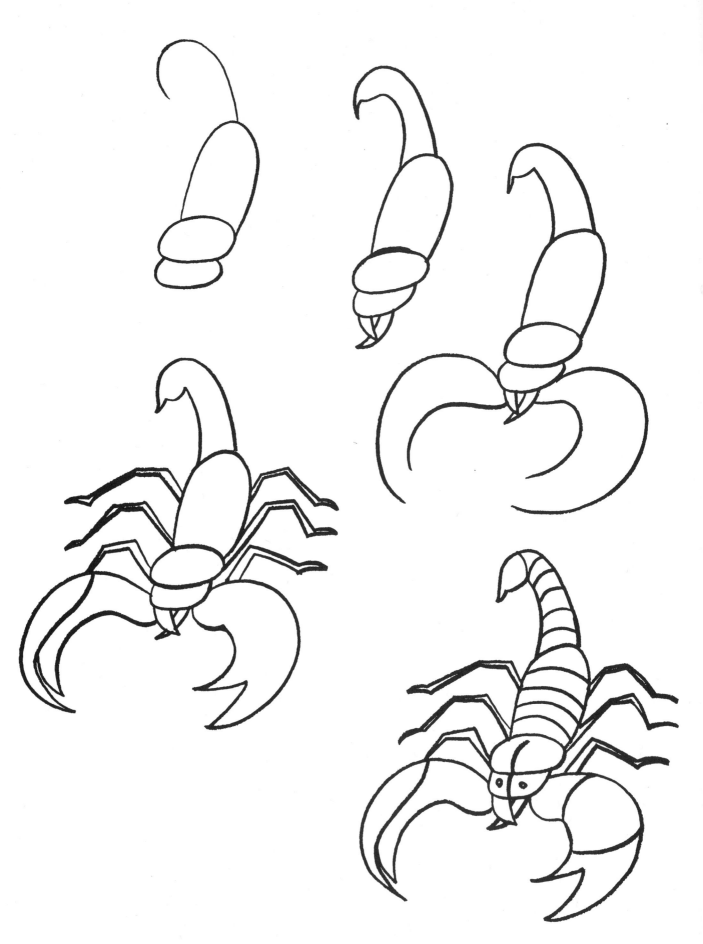

Scorpions have a poisonous sting. They grab smaller victims in their large pincers. Scorpions may be golden brown or gray.

Practice Page

Honeybees are yellow and black. They pollinate plants
and make honey from the pollen they gather.

Practice Page

The queen is the only **bumblebee** that lives through the winter,
in an underground nest. She lays eggs that produce
yellow-and-black worker bees.

Practice Page

Yellow jacket wasps chew wood and build their nests from the pulp.
They are yellow and black.

Practice Page

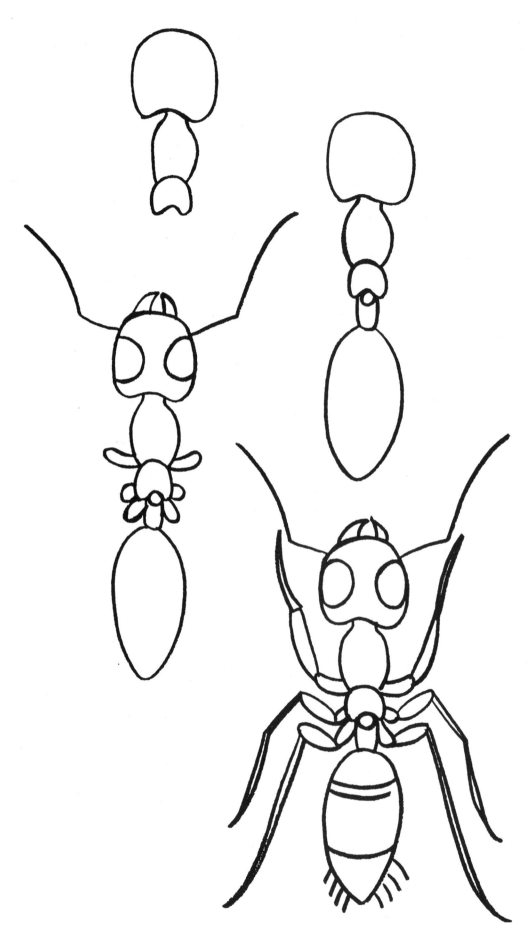

Carpenter ants build their nests in wood—trees, logs, or lumber in buildings. They are brown or black.

Practice Page

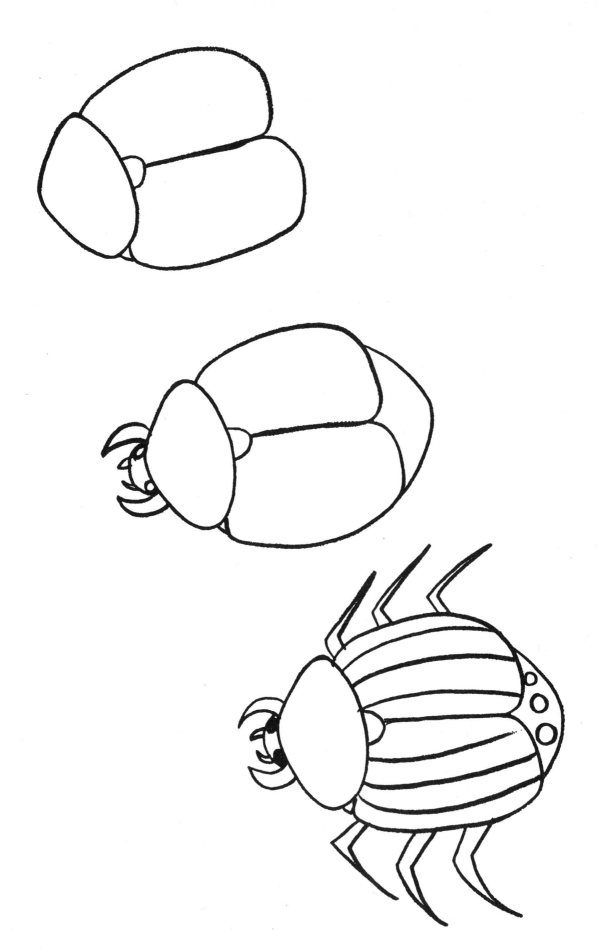

Japanese beetles are bright green and brown.
They eat wood, roots, and grass.

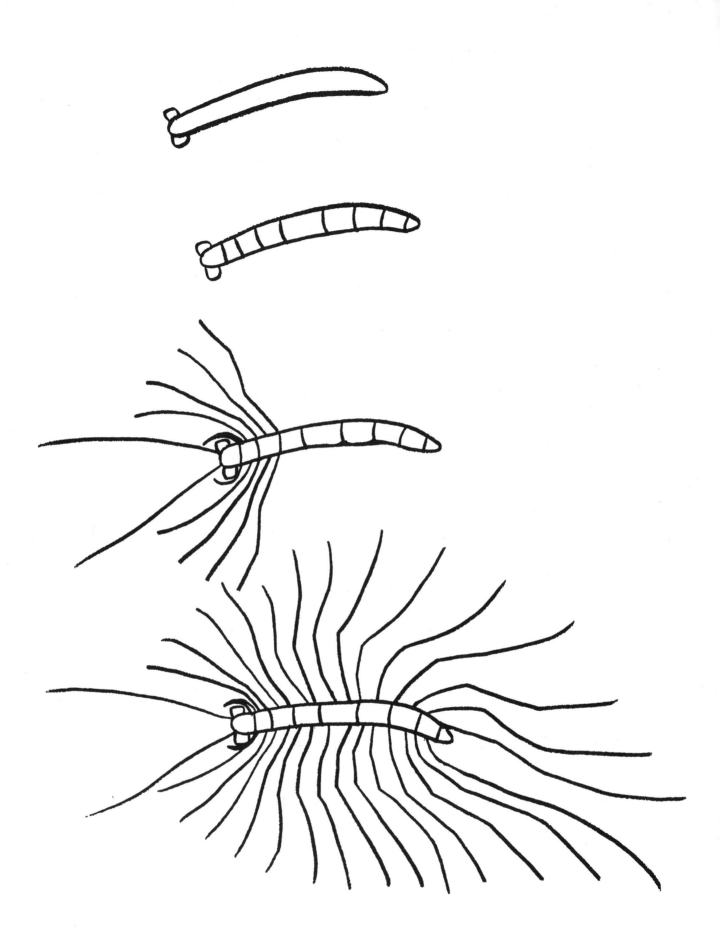

Centipedes are grayish yellow. Their name comes from
the Latin words for "hundred feet." They live indoors in humid
or damp areas such as cellars, bathrooms, closets, and attics.

44

Practice Page

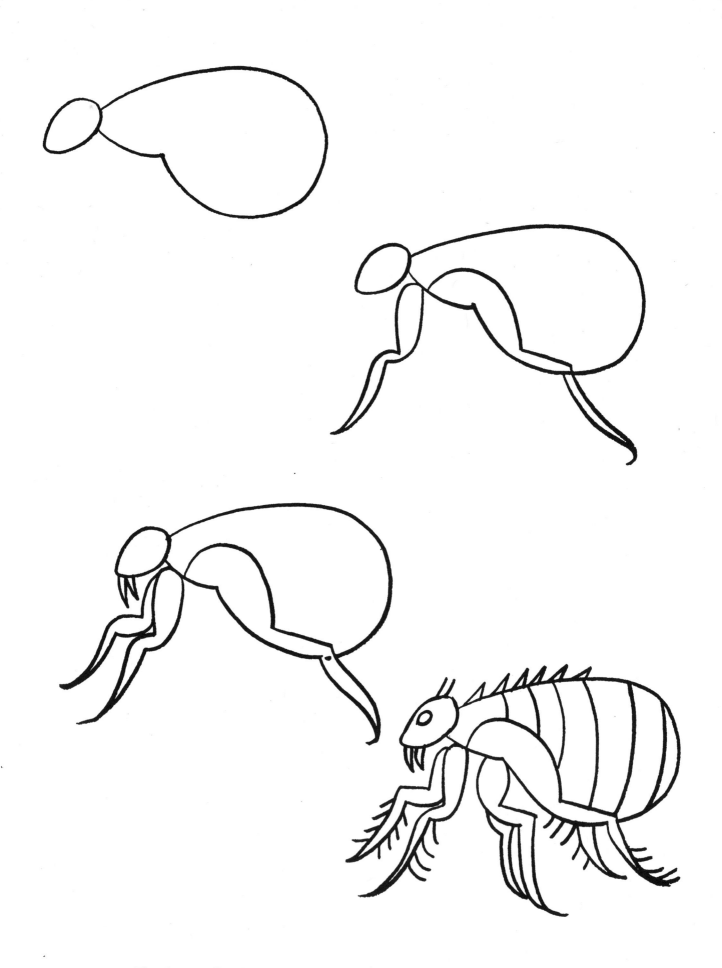

This brown **flea** lives on dogs. It can jump as far as 200 times its length.

Practice Page

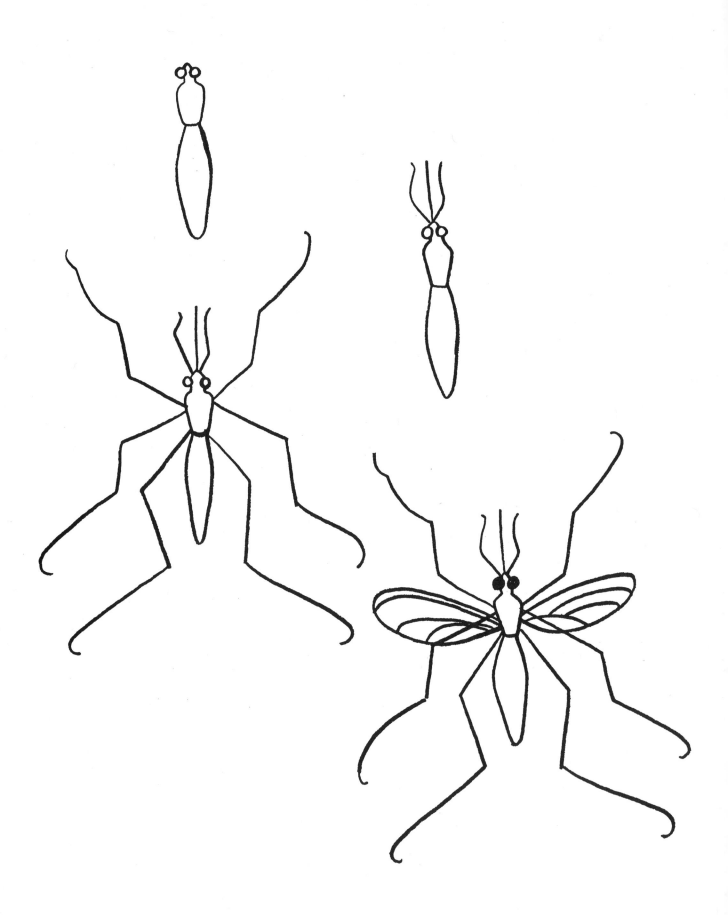

The female **mosquito** bites and buzzes. The male does not.
Some diseases can be spread through mosquito bites.
Mosquitoes are a brownish-red color.

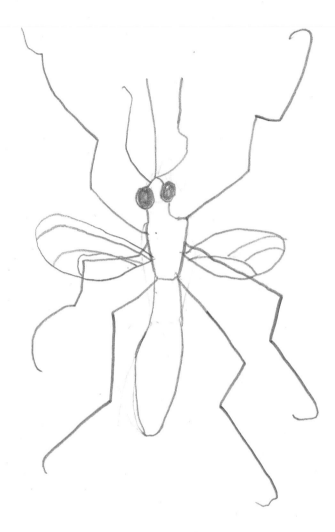

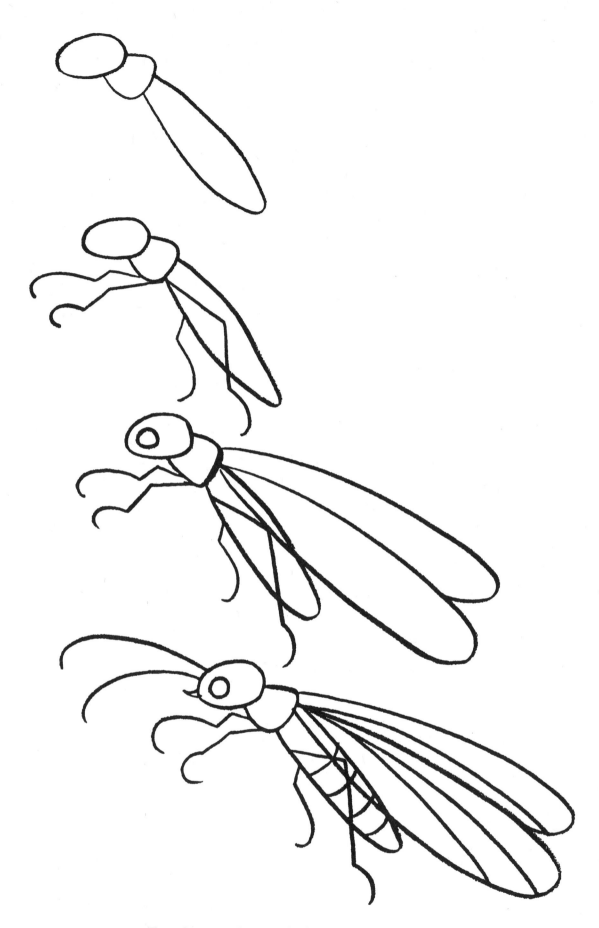

Termites eat the wood of dead trees in the forest.
When they live in a house or other building, they can severely damage
the structure and even cause it to collapse, by eating the wood.

Practice Page

Hornets build oval-shaped nests that hang from trees.
More than 10,000 of them may live in one nest.
Their bodies are black, with some yellow markings.

Practice Page

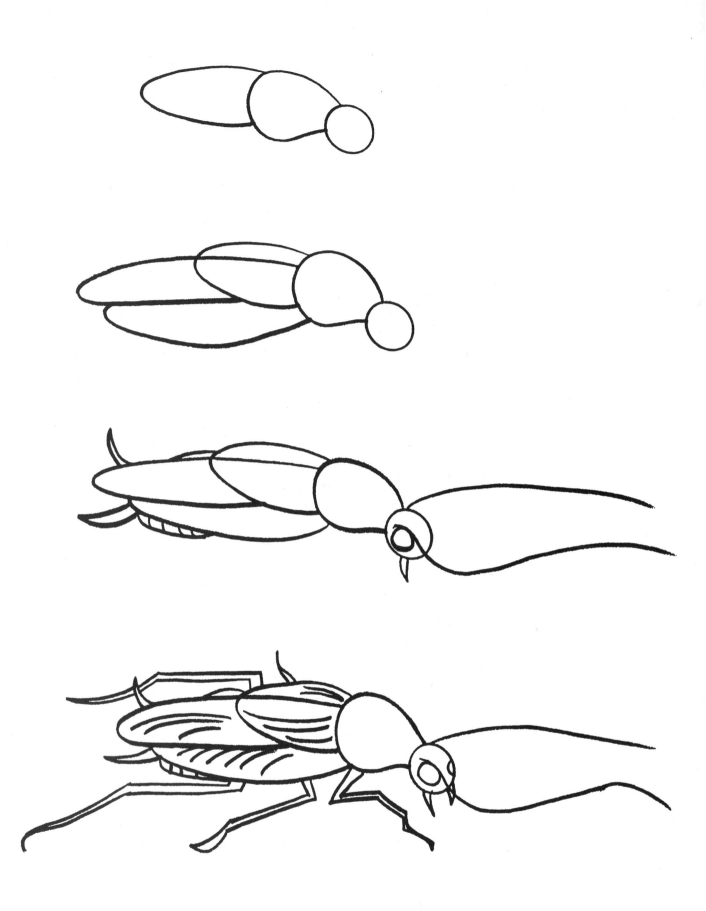

German cockroaches came to the United States from Europe.
They run very fast. Because their bodies are flat,
they can move through the smallest cracks and crevices.

54

Practice Page

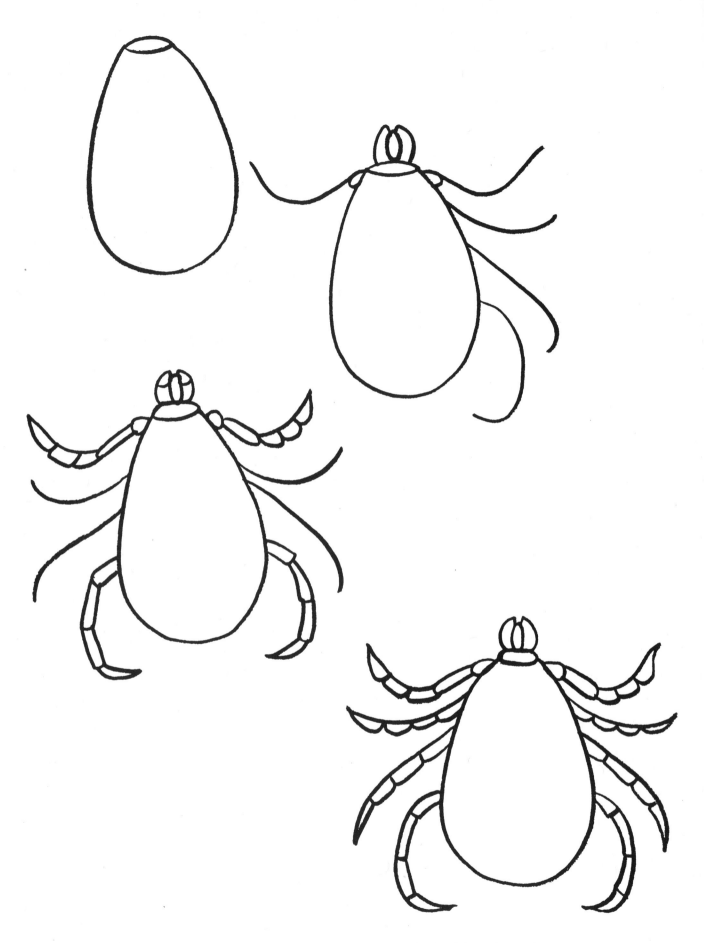

Ticks are parasites. They live on mammals, birds, and reptiles.
They are gray or brown.

Practice Page

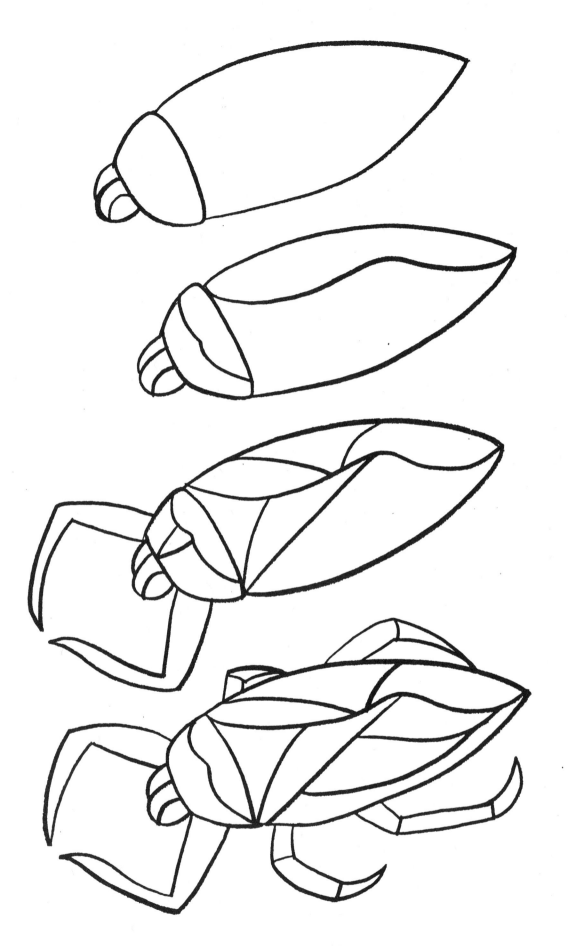

A **giant water bug** may be almost 2½ inches long.
Water bugs can swim underwater and also can fly. They are brown.

Practice Page

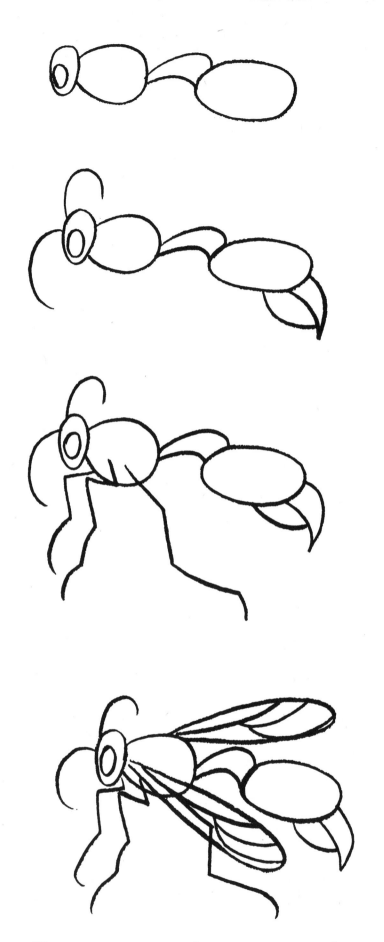

Wasps eat many insects that are pests to people,
but wasps also sting people sometimes. They are social insects
that live in large colonies, as bees and ants do.

Practice Page